AF228623

Alaska

BY AUDREY HARRISON

CONTENT CONSULTANT
Thomas Michael Swensen, PhD (Alutiiq)
Assistant Professor, Ethnic Studies
University of Utah

Core Library

An Imprint of Abdo Publishing
abdobooks.com

abdobooks.com

Published by Abdo Publishing, a division of ABDO, PO Box 398166, Minneapolis, Minnesota 55439.
Copyright © 2023 by Abdo Consulting Group, Inc. International copyrights reserved in all countries.
No part of this book may be reproduced in any form without written permission from the publisher.
Core Library™ is a trademark and logo of Abdo Publishing.

Printed in the United States of America, North Mankato, Minnesota.
052022
092022

Cover Photo: Shutterstock Images
Interior Photos: Natty C./Shutterstock Images, 4–5; Red Line Editorial, 9 (Alaska), 9 (USA); Andy
Kazie/iStockphoto, 10–11; Steven Kazlowski/Nature Picture Library/Alamy, 13; Shutterstock Images,
16 (flag), 16 (dog), 16 (flower), 20–21, 32; Sophia Granchinho/Shutterstock Images, 16 (bird); NPS
Photo/Alamy, 16 (whale); Mike Redwine/Shutterstock Images, 23, 45; Education Images/Universal
Images Group/Getty Images, 26; Sam Chadwick/Shutterstock Images, 28–29, 43; Alaska and Polar
Regions Collections and Archives/University of Alaska Fairbanks/Yvonne Mozee Collection/UAF-
2002-98-13, 34; Shutterstock Images, 34–35; Rob Stapleton/AP/Shutterstock Images, 39; The Asahi
Shimbun/Getty Images, 40

Editor: Katharine Hale
Series Designer: Joshua Olson

Library of Congress Control Number: 2021951406

Publisher's Cataloging-in-Publication Data

Names: Harrison, Audrey, author.
Title: Alaska / by Audrey Harrison
Description: Minneapolis, Minnesota : Abdo Publishing, 2023 | Series: Core library of US states |
        Includes online resources and index.
Identifiers: ISBN 9781532197437 (lib. bdg.) | ISBN 9781098270193 (ebook)
Subjects: LCSH: U.S. states--Juvenile literature. | Western States (U.S.)--Juvenile literature. | Alaska--
        History--Juvenile literature. | Physical geography--United States--Juvenile literature.
Classification: DDC 979.8--dc23

Population demographics broken down by race and ethnicity come from the 2019 census estimate.
Population totals come from the 2020 census.

CONTENTS

THE LAST FRONTIER

A girl stepped onto the Matanuska Glacier. She was glad for her thick jacket and hiking boots. She could see steep mountain peaks in the distance. The girl and her family hiked along the glacier. They squeezed between walls of ice. She felt small compared to the towering chunks of the glacier.

It was hard to believe the glacier was less than three hours away from Anchorage. Anchorage is the largest city in Alaska.

The Matanuska Glacier is the largest glacier in the United States that is accessible by car.

Nearly half of the state's population lives in this city. The girl couldn't wait to explore the city life and the other natural wonders that Alaska had to offer.

EXPLORING ALASKA

The Last Frontier is Alaska's nickname. That's because it is hundreds of miles from the nearest US state. Alaska is also the biggest state. Much of it is wilderness. Some of the wilderness is protected by the US government. These areas of land are protected from being developed or used for resources.

Alaska is located in the extreme northwest of North America.

THE MEANING OF ALASKA

The name Alaska comes from the Unangam Tunuu word *alaxsxaq*. It means "the object toward which the action of the sea is directed." It refers to the Alaskan Peninsula. Alaska is home to many Alaska Native and American Indian peoples, including the Unangax̂ (Aleut). The state is nearly surrounded by seas and oceans. The seas and the food they provide are an important part of Alaskan culture.

Canada borders the state to the east. Alaska's southern and western coasts are on the Pacific Ocean. The Arctic Ocean and Beaufort Sea lie to the north of the state. At one spot, the mainland of Alaska is only 55 miles (89 km) from Russia's mainland. The mainland states, which many Alaskans call the Lower 48, are many times farther away.

The Alaskan Peninsula juts out from the southwestern part of the state. It is one of the largest peninsulas in the world. Bristol Bay and the Bering Sea are above the peninsula. The Gulf of Alaska

PERSPECTIVES

BOB ROSS

Bob Ross was an American painter who was known for his TV show *The Joy of Painting*. The show taught people how to paint. Ross was known for his positivity and gentle instructions. Ross was born in Florida. But his work for the US Air Force brought him to Alaska. He said on his show that he had never seen snow before living in Alaska. While there, he fell in love with the state. Many of his paintings included Alaskan settings. Ross said, "If you have never been to Alaska, go there while it is still wild."

and Pacific Ocean are below. There are several fishing villages located on the Alaskan Peninsula, including King Cove and Sand Point. Many of the people who live in this region year-round are Alaska Natives. In some areas, Alaska Natives make up more than 60 percent of the population. Most visitors to the Alaskan Peninsula come to see the region's volcanoes and wildlife. Several national parks and nature preserves are there. They protect plants and animals, such as brown bears.

The majority of Alaska's population lives in several large cities, including Anchorage, Fairbanks, and Juneau. Juneau is Alaska's capital. In the past it had three of the world's largest gold mines. Today people visit the state for many reasons. They enjoy outdoor activities or see museums. Like the nickname suggests, Alaska offers lots of land to explore.

MAP OF
ALASKA

Alaska has many important cities and famous landmarks. What does this map show you about the locations of Alaska's major cities? How does this map help you understand Alaska's unique geography?

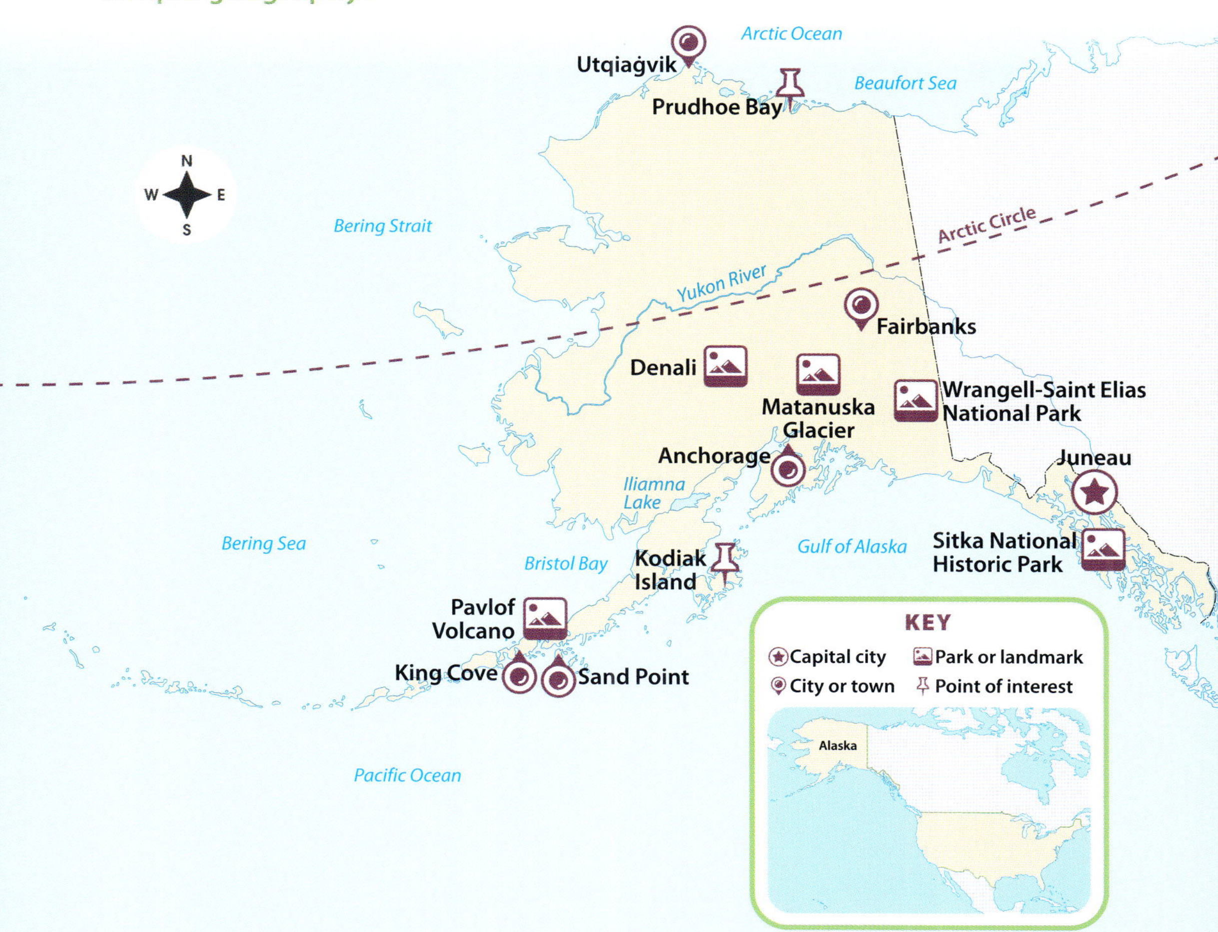

HISTORY OF ALASKA

People have been living in Alaska for more than 12,000 years. Historians aren't sure how the first people arrived. One popular theory is that early people crossed a land bridge from what is now Russia. The Bering Strait lies between Russia and Alaska, but sea levels were once lower. Some scientists think that there was an area of land that people could walk across. Other people may have come to the region by boat. Over time, sea levels rose, and the land

Scientists believe ancient people arrived in present-day Alaska via the Bering Strait. They may have come on a land bridge or by boat.

bridge was covered. Scientists believe that early people continued to arrive over thousands of years.

Alaska Native peoples settled in different regions of the state. The Tlingit, Haida, and Tsimshian nations lived in the southeastern region. These peoples lived in forests. The Tlingit and Haida used cedar trees for baskets and utensils. They also used cedar for totem poles and canoes. Totem poles represent family histories or important events. Canoes allowed these peoples to hunt for fish and trade with nearby nations.

The Athabascan peoples lived in the interior portion of Alaska, away from the coasts. The Athabascans consist of many nations. They were known for their hunting skills, which included tracking caribou through the harsh environment. Temperatures in this region could reach −50 degrees Fahrenheit (−46°C).

The Yupik homeland is in southwestern Alaska. These peoples wore animal furs to survive the extreme cold. They lived in partly underground shelters.

Some Alaska Natives, including the Inupiaq, continue to use skin-covered canoes to hunt whales.

The Yupik were experienced hunters, capable of taking down whales from their animal skin–covered canoes. Today there are several nations with Yupik ancestry.

The Unangax̂ (Aleut) were also known for their skills at sea. *Unangax̂* translates to "seasiders." Much of the Unangax̂'s tools, food, and shelter came from sea animals such as whales and fish.

Alaska Natives continue to make up a large portion of Alaska's population and identity today. Some Alaska Natives continue to eat traditional foods. Native cultures are still celebrated in ceremonies and art.

RUSSIAN ARRIVAL

Russian fur traders first reached Alaska in 1741. They discovered the land had many animals that could be killed for their fur, including seals and sea otters. The Russians relied on getting fur pelts from the Unangax̂ people. Russians sometimes threatened the Unangax̂. They also took some Unangax̂ people as hostages. The nation had to provide pelts in exchange for their people. The Unangax̂ repeatedly tried to fight back, but they were unable to drive the Russians from their land. The Alutiiq faced similar treatment.

Gradually the Russians began making less money from the fur trade. Sea otters were almost completely wiped out due to the industry. The Russian government approached the US government about selling Alaska to the United States.

US Secretary of State William Seward agreed to purchase Alaska from Russia. The $7.2 million purchase was finalized in April 1867. Seward believed Alaska would give the United States easier access to trade with China and Japan. Gold was first discovered in Alaska in 1872. More gold was found in the Klondike River in 1896. This is in the Yukon Territory in Canada, near Alaska. More than 100,000 people traveled north hoping to get rich.

The Klondike Gold Rush had a negative effect on Indigenous peoples in Alaska and Canada. Gold mining supplies arrived by boat on

FIGHTING FOR EQUALITY

Elizabeth Peratrovich helped get the first antidiscrimination act passed in Alaska. She was a member of the Tlingit nation. Alaska Natives and people of color were treated unfairly. The state had separate schools, restaurants, and hospitals for Alaska Natives and white people. Some business owners even hung "no natives allowed" signs in their windows. In the early 1940s, Peratrovich wrote to Alaska's governor. She pointed out the unfair treatment. Peratrovich's first attempt to change the law failed. But the Antidiscrimination Bill of 1945 eventually passed on February 16 of that year. It banned racial discrimination in public places in Alaska.

QUICK FACTS

Alaska has many different wilderness areas. What do the state symbols of Alaska show you about the diversity of the state's landscapes?

Abbreviation: AK
Nickname: The Last Frontier
Motto: North to the future
Date of statehood: January 3, 1959
Capital: Juneau
Population: 733,391
Area: 665,384 square miles (1,723,337 sq km)

STATE SYMBOLS

State bird
Willow
ptarmigan

State flower
Alpine forget-
me-not

State dog
Alaskan
malamute

**State marine
mammal**
Bowhead
whale

the Yukon River. This damaged the river's health and hurt Indigenous people's fish supply. Gold seekers overhunted animals such as moose and caribou, which Indigenous people depended on for food.

Alaska Natives also faced discrimination from the US government. American Indians and Alaska Natives were not considered US citizens until 1924. They were not allowed to vote or own property. The US government even tried to stop Alaska Natives from speaking their native languages.

STATEHOOD

On January 3, 1959, Alaska became the forty-ninth US state. Another population boom happened after statehood. Oil was discovered at Prudhoe Bay in 1968. Soon after, oil surpassed gold and other minerals as the most important natural resource.

Today Alaska's state government has three branches. The executive branch is led by the governor. The House of Representatives and the Senate make up

PERSPECTIVES

OIL AND ALASKA NATIVE CULTURE

Government officials believed Alaska could be a good source of energy. The land had oil. In August 2020, the US government approved a plan. It would open 1.56 million acres (631,300 ha) of Alaska's coast for oil drilling. Some people worried about the effect this would have on the environment. Oil drilling could hurt wildlife. Less wildlife would limit the food supplies of Alaska Natives. Gwich'in member Bernadette Demientieff believed the plan disrespected Alaska Native cultures. She said, "Our ways of life, our food security, and our identity is not up for negotiation."

the legislative branch. The judicial branch is the court system, which reviews laws.

Alaska residents have grappled with important issues in Alaska's short history as a US state. The United States had purchased Alaska from Russia. But Alaska Natives never gave their lands to Russia. In 1971 President Richard Nixon signed the Alaska Native Claims Settlement Act. It returned 45.5 million acres (18.4 million ha) of land to Alaska Natives.

STRAIGHT TO THE SOURCE

By signing the Russian Treaty, the United States officially purchased Alaska from Russia. Not everyone thought this was a good deal. An 1867 article in the *New York Tribune* criticized Secretary of State William Seward for the purchase:

> *What will the government of this ice-covered desert cost? It was stated at the War Department . . . that it would require a regiment of infantry. It costs $1,100 a year to maintain a single soldier in Washington[, DC]. It would cost twice as much in Seward's desert. It costs $1,000,000 a year to keep a man-of-war [ship] at sea. We should have to have at least six on the 3,000 miles [4,800 km] of Seward's coast, as naval men say here. We should have to institute a territorial government. What wouldn't that cost?*

> Source: "Washington: The Russian Treaty." *New York Tribune*, vol. XXVI, no. 8,112, 9 Apr. 1867, chroniclingamerica.loc.gov. Accessed 16 Feb. 2021.

CHANGING MINDS

Imagine you supported the purchase of Alaska from Russia. What would you say in response to this article? Make sure you explain your opinion. Include facts and details that support your reasons.

GEOGRAPHY AND CLIMATE

From the islands to the mainland, Alaska has a variety of land and water features. The state is home to 17 of the top 20 tallest peaks in the United States. Alaska has thousands of miles of coastline and approximately 100,000 glaciers. There are 3,000 rivers and 3 million lakes in the state. Iliamna Lake is the state's largest lake, at 1,150 square miles (3,000 sq km) in area.

Alaska is a large state with multiple climates. Temperatures are generally colder

Alaska has the most lakes of any US state.

in the north than in the south. Higher altitudes also have colder temperatures. Mountains block rain and snow from falling in certain areas of the state. This causes regions of Alaska to have varying amounts of precipitation. Some areas of Alaska have frequent blizzards, while others remain dry year-round.

TUNDRA AND FORESTS

Tundra is cold, treeless landscape that gets little rain. It lines Alaska's northern and western coasts. Utqiaġvik, Alaska, is located in the tundra. It receives only approximately 4 inches (10 cm) of rain or snow every year.

In the northern regions, nearly 85 percent of the ground is permafrost. This means that the top layer of soil is always frozen. In warmer parts of the state, frozen soil may melt in the summer. This allows Arctic grasses and wildflowers to sprout up.

More than 1,000 islands dot southeast Alaska. They get a lot of rain. Off the southwest peninsula, 69 islands

rise out of the water. Weather there is wet, stormy, and foggy. The peninsula stretches 500 miles (800 km) into the Pacific. A range of volcanoes stand along the edge. Pavlof Volcano is the most active.

On Alaska's mainland, flat wetlands cover the south and central regions. The ground freezes and melts each year. Forests grow there. Black and white spruces mix with other evergreen trees, along with cedar, aspen, and birch trees.

Plants and animals that live in Alaska must be able to survive cold habitats. Nearly one-third of the state is located in the Arctic Circle. This is the northernmost region of the world. Mammals such as hares, caribou, and seals live near the Arctic Circle. These animals rely on layers of fat to protect them from the cold. Birds including sparrows, puffins, and albatross fly through the skies. Clams, crabs, and shrimp live in ocean waters. Alaska's state marine mammal, the bowhead whale, is found in the Arctic Ocean.

WHALES

Fourteen types of whales swim in Alaskan waters. The humpback whale is one. Adult females often measure 49 feet (15 m) long. The North Pacific right whale is even larger. It is mainly found in the Bering Sea and the North Pacific Ocean. The beluga swims in the Arctic Ocean. It is small compared to other whales. It uses echolocation to learn about its surroundings and to hunt for food.

THREATENED BY CLIMATE CHANGE

Climate change threatens all parts of Alaska. This is the gradual warming of Earth's temperatures. It is caused by human activities that release harmful gases into the air. These gases trap heat in Earth's atmosphere. Warmer temperatures can lead to extreme weather and earthquakes.

Alaska is located in one of the most at-risk areas for earthquakes in the world. On March 27, 1964, an earthquake struck southeastern Alaska. It was the most powerful earthquake in

PERSPECTIVES

TSUNAMIS

Some towns in Alaska experience tsunamis. Tsunamis are long, tall sea waves. They can be caused by landslides. Large pieces of rock and ice fall into the sea from the mountains. The impact creates a huge wave. It can be deadly. Glaciers have been melting due to climate change. The land underneath is unstable. This makes landslides more likely. Bretwood Higman is a scientist in Alaska. He said, "[Tsunamis] are worth worrying about regardless of climate change. But there are a number of reasons to think climate change makes them a lot more likely."

Kodiak, *pictured*, suffered major damage after the 1964 earthquake. The resulting tsunami caused damage as far away as Crescent City, California.

US history and the second-most powerful earthquake in recorded history. It caused a lot of damage.

Scientists have recorded melting ice in Alaska since 1979. This raises sea levels. It takes away wildlife habitats. Animals such as polar bears struggle to survive. They depend on ice to hunt.

Rising temperatures also affect the people living in the state. Melting permafrost can damage the structure of buildings and roads. Rising sea levels threaten to wipe out coastal cities and towns. Climate experts work to pass laws that would reduce harmful activities that cause climate change. They work with lawmakers to increase the use of clean energy, such as solar and wind energy, within the state.

FURTHER EVIDENCE

Chapter Three discusses Alaska's geography and the unique animals and plants that live in the state. What was one of the main points of this chapter? What evidence is included to support this point? Read the article at the website below. Does the information on the website support the main point of the chapter? Does it present new evidence?

WILDLIFE VIEWING

abdocorelibrary.com/alaska

RESOURCES AND ECONOMY

One of Alaska's main resources is oil. It has been a major part of the economy since 1968, when it was discovered in Prudhoe Bay. Construction began on the Trans-Alaska Pipeline soon after the discovery. The pipeline connected oil fields in northern Prudhoe Bay to Valdez. Valdez is 800 miles (1,290 km) south of the bay. The pipeline was completed on May 31, 1977.

Soon after the pipeline opened, the state government created the Alaska

Some Trans-Alaska Pipeline pipes are raised high off the ground so the pipes don't melt permafrost and so animals can walk underneath.

Permanent Fund. This fund pays each resident a sum of money every year. The amount depends on how much oil is produced. No other state has an economic fund like this. But the pipeline has risks. Major oil spills in 1989 and 2006 harmed wildlife.

PERSPECTIVES

FISHING INDUSTRY

Commercial fishing can hurt the environment. It can destroy fish habitats. Certain species may be overfished. Linda Behnken is a commercial fisher and the director of the Alaska Longline Fishermen's Association. She won an award for her work to reduce the environmental effects of commercial fishing. Most people working in this industry are men. But Behnken was drawn to the work. She said, "One of the things that attracted me to fishing is it's not anything about what you look like or other aspects of you—it's what you can do when you're working first as crew."

WILDLIFE AND TOURISM

The fishing industry is another part of Alaska's economy. Salmon fishing is especially important. More than 100 million pink salmon are caught or farmed each year. Shellfish are the second-most important creatures to the fishing industry. They include crabs, shrimp, scallops, and clams. The Bering Sea is the best place to catch shellfish.

Approximately 10 percent of Alaska's workforce has a tourism-related job. Alaska gets more than 1 million visitors each year. People enjoy cruises and beautiful scenery. Alaska is also home to eight national parks. The US National Park Service reported that these parks had more than 2.9 million visits in 2018. National parks alone brought in nearly $2 billion to the tourism industry in 2018.

LARGEST NATIONAL PARK

Wrangell-Saint Elias National Park and Preserve is the largest national park in the United States. It has more than 13.2 million acres (5.3 million ha) to explore. This is approximately six times larger than Yellowstone National Park, which is mostly in Wyoming. Visitors enjoy stunning landscapes. They can see glaciers and volcanoes. This park is also home to many animals such as grizzly bears and caribou.

In the early 2000s, nearly 66 percent of Alaskan workers had government jobs. Some people worked in state or local government. The number of military positions has also increased since the opening of a US Air Force base in 1991.

Other parts of Alaska's economy include hydropower and agriculture. Hydropower is getting electricity from rushing water. Alaska has lots of waterways. This energy source could become more widely used in the future. Alaska also influences space exploration. The Pacific Spaceport Complex on Kodiak Island is a launch site for rockets. From wildlife and tourism to energy and space technology, Alaska's economy covers a wide range of sectors.

STRAIGHT TO THE
SOURCE

In March 2019 the University of Alaska analyzed the economic impact of outdoor activities in Alaska. They presented their findings to the Alaska government:

Of all 50 states, Alaska has the lowest population density, greatest acreage of wilderness areas, and highest rates of participation in many outdoor activities. A majority of Alaskans say that opportunities to get outside are a reason they choose to live or remain in the state, and a similar share of visitors come to Alaska to experience the great outdoors. Both locals and visitors spend money in the course of their activities that circulates throughout the state economy, making outdoor recreation a substantial industry.

Source: University of Alaska Center for Economic Development. *Outdoor Recreation: Impacts and Opportunities*. Mar. 2019, commerce.alaska.gov. PDF. Accessed 11 Mar. 2021.

WHAT'S THE BIG IDEA

Take a close look at this passage. What is the main connection being made between Alaska and the outdoors? What makes Alaska special to residents and tourists?

PEOPLE AND PLACES

Many notable people have come from Alaska. Walter Harper was a Koyukon-Athabascan who was born in 1892. He is famous for being the first person to reach the peak of Denali. At 20,320 feet (6,194 m) above sea level, Denali is the highest peak in North America.

Benny Benson is another notable Alaskan. He was born in Chignik in 1913. His father was Swedish, and his mother was Unangax̂-Russian. In 1926, the governor of the Alaska Territory

Walter Harper was the first person to climb Denali. He was part of the Karstens-Stuck Expedition in 1913.

was fighting for statehood. He thought Alaska needed a flag. He helped create a contest where Alaskan students could design a flag. Benny was in seventh grade when he won the contest. The flag was officially adopted in 1927. This was only a few years after Alaska Natives were considered citizens. Benny became a source of pride for many Alaska Natives. Benny received a scholarship and a watch with the new flag's design as his prize.

DEMOGRAPHICS

Approximately 65 percent of Alaska's population is white. European culture is visible within the state. Russians occupied Alaska for nearly 125 years. Their influence can still be seen in historic Russian buildings.

Alaska Natives make up nearly 16 percent of Alaska's population. There are 229 Alaska Native tribes that are recognized by the US government. This is nearly half of all tribal nations recognized by the United States. The Central Alaskan Yupik is the largest Alaska

Native nation in the state today. And the Yupik language is the most widely spoken of Alaska Native languages. Alaska's official languages are English and 20 Alaska Native languages. Alaska Natives live throughout many regions, and each nation celebrates its own unique culture.

Alaska Native influence is noticeable in the arts. Wood and ivory carving come from some traditions. Beadwork and basket weaving are also common art forms. Some Alaska Native nations also celebrate their cultures

PERSPECTIVES

ALASKA NATIVE HERITAGE CENTER

The Alaska Native Heritage Center (ANHC) is located in Anchorage. In 2020 the cultural center was awarded $3 million from the Ford Foundation. ANHC planned to use the funds to further develop a space for Indigenous people to celebrate their cultures. Emily Edenshaw was the executive director of ANHC in 2020. She also joined the Alaska Tourism Industry Association Board of Directors. She said, "Alaska always has and always will be a Native place, and our tourism industry needs to reflect this fact."

DOGSLED RACING CHAMP

Susan Butcher enjoyed dogsled racing and raising huskies in Alaska. Starting in 1986, she won the Iditarod Race four times in five years. The famous Iditarod starts in Anchorage. It ends in Nome. It is about 1,100 miles (1,770 km) long. Competitors cross two mountain ranges and many frozen waterways. Butcher's fastest time was 10 days, 22 hours, and 2 minutes.

through sport. The World Eskimo-Indian Olympic Games are held in Fairbanks. *Eskimo* is a term that some Alaska Natives use to refer to themselves. But some Indigenous people consider the term offensive, especially when used by people outside the culture. During the games, Indigenous people from Alaska, Canada, and Greenland compete in traditional challenges. These challenges test a competitor's strength and endurance. One competition is the ear weight. A man hangs 16 pounds (7.3 kg) from his ear.

Susan Butcher became the first person to win the Iditarod Trail Dog Sled Race three consecutive years, in 1986, 1987, *pictured*, and 1988. She won again in 1990.

AMERICA'S TIME.
02:25:02
Courtesy of 24 KARAT ALASKA JEWELERS
IDITAROD CHAMPION
PRO

From the Iditarod Race to the northern lights, *pictured*, to glaciers and lakes, there is something for everyone in Alaska.

He carries it as far as possible. The test shows his ability to handle pain such as frostbite.

SIGHTSEEING

Sitka National Historic Park is the oldest federally recognized park in Alaska. The park highlights totem poles, an example of Native art. These poles are part of the Tlingit and Haida cultures, among others. Totem poles were made to celebrate a person's achievements or to record important historical events.

Some represent families or Native religions. A collection of totem poles has been preserved at Sitka National Historic Park. The Sitka tribe began working with the park in 2018 to ensure that Alaska Native representation is accurate.

Natural wonders attract many people to Alaska. At certain times of the year, people can see the northern lights. They see streaks of green and red in the sky. The state has many national parks and sites. Visitors can hike or ride cruise ships. As the last frontier, Alaska offers new experiences each day.

EXPLORE ONLINE

Chapter Five discusses the World Eskimo-Indian Olympic Games. The site below describes events that take place during this competition. What do the events show you about the histories and cultures today of some Alaska Native peoples?

THE WEIO GAMES
abdocorelibrary.com/alaska

IMPORTANT DATES

12,000 years ago
People first arrive in Alaska.

1741
Russian fur traders first arrive in Alaska.

1867
In April, US Secretary of State William Seward purchases Alaska from Russia for $7.2 million.

1945
Alaska's first antidiscrimination bill is passed on February 16. It bans discrimination in public places.

1959
Alaska becomes the forty-ninth state on January 3.

1964
An earthquake occurs in southeastern Alaska on March 27. It goes on record as the most powerful earthquake in US history.

1968

Oil is discovered in Prudhoe Bay.

1977

Construction of the Trans-Alaska Pipeline System is completed on May 31.

Say What?

Learning about state history and geography can mean learning a lot of new vocabulary. Find five words in this book you've never heard before. Use a dictionary to find out what they mean. Then write the meanings in your own words and use each word in a new sentence.

You Are There

This book describes some of Alaska's national parks. Imagine you are visiting Wrangell-Saint Elias. Write a letter home telling your friends what you have seen. What do you notice about the landscape and wildlife? Be sure to add plenty of detail to your notes.

Tell the Tale

Chapter Four describes important parts of Alaska's economy, such as tourism. Imagine you are a tour guide in Alaska. Write 200 words about why people should come visit the state. What makes Alaska special?

Another View

This book talks about how climate change affects Alaska's geography. As you know, every source is different. Ask a librarian or another adult to help you find another source about this topic. Write a short essay comparing and contrasting the new source's point of view with that of this book's author. What is the point of view of each author? How are they similar and why? How are they different and why?

GLOSSARY

agriculture
the practice of farming crops and livestock

discrimination
when people treat others differently based on certain factors such as appearance

echolocation
the ability to locate objects using sound

frostbite
damage of body parts due to cold temperatures

glacier
a large body of ice that moves across land

habitat
the place where a plant or animal lives

hostage
a person who is taken by another person or group to be exchanged for items or money

Indigenous
relating to the earliest known residents of an area

peninsula
a body of land that is surrounded by water on three sides

ONLINE RESOURCES

To learn more about Alaska, visit our free resource websites below.

Visit **abdocorelibrary.com** or scan this QR code for free Common Core resources for teachers and students, including vetted activities, multimedia, and booklinks, for deeper subject comprehension.

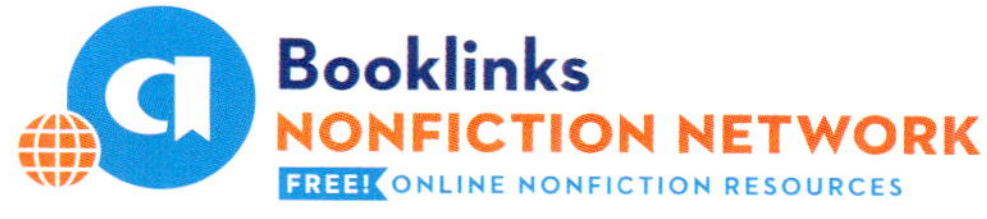

Visit **abdobooklinks.com** or scan this QR code for free additional online weblinks for further learning. These links are routinely monitored and updated to provide the most current information available.

LEARN MORE

Brown, Tricia. *Children of the First People: Fresh Voices of Alaska's Native Kids*. West Margin, 2019.

Yasuda, Anita. *Exploring the West*. Abdo, 2018.

INDEX

About the Author

Audrey Harrison lives in Minnesota. She enjoys mystery novels and jigsaw puzzles. She has visited 32 states and counting.